Classic Recipes of
NORWAY

Classic Recipes of
NORWAY

TRADITIONAL FOOD AND COOKING
IN 25 AUTHENTIC DISHES

JANET LAURENCE

LORENZ BOOKS

This edition is published by Lorenz Books
an imprint of Anness Publishing Ltd
info@anness.com
annesspublishing.com

If you like the images in this book
and would like to investigate using
them for publishing, promotions or
advertising, please visit our website
www.practicalpictures.com for more
information.

Publisher: Joanna Lorenz
Editorial Director: Helen Sudell
Designer: Nigel Partridge
Recipe Photography: William Lingwood
Food Stylist: Fergal Connolly
Prop Stylist: Helent Trent
Production Controller: Ben Worley

PUBLISHER'S NOTE
Although the advice and information in this
book are believed to be accurate and true
at the time of going to press, neither the
authors nor the publisher can accept any
legal responsibility or liability for any errors
or omissions that may have been made nor
for any inaccuracies nor for any loss, harm
or injury that comes about from following
instructions or advice in this book.

PUBLISHER'S ACKNOWLEDGMENTS
The Publisher would like to thank the
following agencies for the use of their
images. Alamy: p10tr, p11. Superstock: 6,
9, 10bl, 13, 15bl.

COOK'S NOTES
Bracketed terms are intended for American
readers. For all recipes, quantities are
given in both metric and imperial measures
and, where appropriate, in standard
cups and spoons. Follow one set of
measures, but not a mixture, because
they are not interchangeable.

Standard spoon and cup measures are
level. 1 tsp = 5ml, 1 tbsp = 15ml, 1
cup = 250ml/8fl oz. Australian standard
tablespoons are 20ml. Australian readers
should use 3 tsp in place of 1 tbsp for
measuring small quantities.

American pints are 16fl oz/2 cups.
American readers should use 20fl oz/
2.5 cups in place of 1 pint when measuring
liquids.

Electric oven temperatures in this book
are for conventional ovens. When using
a fan oven, the temperature will probably
need to be reduced by about 10–20°C/
20–40°F. Since ovens vary, you should
check with your manufacturer's instruction
book for guidance.

The nutritional analysis given for each
recipe is calculated per portion (i.e.
serving or item), unless otherwise stated.
If the recipe gives a range, such as Serves
4–6, then the nutritional analysis will be
for the smaller portion size, i.e. 6 servings.
The analysis does not include optional
ingredients, such as salt added to taste.

Medium (US large) eggs are used unless
otherwise stated.

Contents

Introduction

Norway is a fantastical land of soaring mountains, peaceful valleys, silver lakes, and rushing rivers. Despite seasonal extremes, where for half of the year much of the country is covered in snow, nature is generous in Norway. Both salt and fresh waters teem with high-quality fish; the agricultural land available is fertile and produces fine crops; and sheep or goats feed on green pastures above the deep fjords. The Norwegian attitude to food is deeply bound up in the landscape and the necessity of ensuring the produce of the short summer is preserved to last through the long winter. Creative ways of using ingredients to make them taste good all year round defines Norwegian cuisine.

Left: The picturesque fishing village of Reine by the fjord on Lofoten Island.

Norwegian Cuisine

Traditional cooking in Norway stems from its peasant culture; a simple, wholesome diet where food was harvested from sea and land. Families who lived along the coast would be both fishermen and farmers. As a result, the Norwegian diet has been defined by livestock, grain and fish, with plentiful supplies of milk, bread and fish, particularly cod and herring.

Below: Norwegians relish the fresh berries that arrive every summer in the countryside.

Preserving for winter

In Norway, food has always been grown and preserved. Vegetables were selected for their ease of storage, such as beetroot (beet) and potatoes. Barley and other grains were great standbys for making sustaining porridge, as well as soups and bread. Domestic cows, sheep and goats were fattened on summer feed and then slaughtered, smoked, salted or wet-cured for the winter months ahead.

Mealtime traditions

A strong farming heritage dictates that classic dishes are based on local produce. Eating well in the morning is essential for all families. *Frokost*, or breakfast, includes *grøt*, a filling porridge of milk and flour, or the richer *rømmegrøt*, with cream and flour. Breakfast also features cold meats and fish, cheese, eggs, stewed fruits and bread with lots of coffee.

Lunchtime is usually a rushed affair of an open sandwich wrapped in special paper called *matpakke*.

The 5pm 'middag' for most people is the only hot meal of the day, consisting of a main dish of meat, seafood or pasta, usually accompanied by potatoes and a small amount of other vegetables. Dishes for this meal might include *fårikål*, a stew with lamb, cabbage and whole peppercorns.

Preserved meat and sausages are available in all regions, and are typically served with sour cream and flat bread.

One of Norway's most recognized fish dishes is smoked salmon, and this is most often served with scrambled eggs and dill or mustard sauce. Then there are the many guises of pickled herring and anchovy, which adorn the main dinner table, as well as being eaten for aftons, an evening snack.

Right: Smoked salmon from Norway is hugely popular and is served in many different ways.

Norwegian Food and Festivals

Festivals in Norway can be traced to the changing seasons, the church calendar and historical influences. They range from the start of the year, when people's fortunes were predicted, to the traditional Christmas festivities.

New Year's Day

This used to be a day of omens when the successful production of crops and food was predicted, as well as the general fortunes for the year ahead. It is still a flag-flying day that is associated with the making of resolutions.

Below: Semla is a delicious Fat Tuesday pastry.

Shrovetide

Fastelavn, or Shrovetide, runs through Shrove Sunday to Shrove Tuesday, or Fat Tuesday, the latter marked by eating a traditional pastry, called semla, filled with marzipan and whipped cream. Although officially celebrating the day before Lent begins, Shrovetide is also a celebration of the approach of spring.

Easter

The year's most important church festival, *Påske*, is sometimes referred to as Quiet Week, linked to the Easter message of the suffering of Jesus and his resurrection from the dead. Now the celebration has lost much of its sober connotations and provides another occasion for days in the mountains, skiing and celebrating. Easter eggs are decorated and rolled down a slope. Easter dishes are typically egg dishes and lamb, the latter originating in the ancient Jewish sacrifice of lambs during Passover.

Above: Two girls carry candles to celebrate Santa Lucia.

Constitution Day

Norway's celebration of its independence falls on 17th May. Breakfast often starts with *spekemat* (cured meats), smoked salmon, scrambled eggs and pickled herrings, as well as stewed fruits, bread and coffee. In Oslo, citizens assemble to greet the royal family and processions are made with school children holding flags and sprays of newly emerged birch leaves.

Midsummer's Eve

Sankhansaften, *Jonsok*, or Midsummer's Eve was an ancient festival to herald the summer solstice. On this night, witches were believed to be abroad, and bonfires were lit up along the coast to protect against evil spirits. Now Jonsok is a private celebration where people have their own bonfires at home.

Santa Lucia day

This custom, which originates in Sweden, is celebrated on 13th December as a feast of light. Dressed in white, young girls wear a crown of lighted candles and offer coffee and buns or cookies.

Christmas

The main Christmas event is held on Christmas Eve when it is common to attend carol services. Norwegians use the traditional celebrations such as the Christmas tree, cards, gifts, and Santa Claus, plus the more ancient influence of the Norwegian *Fjøsnisse* (goblin

who lives in the barn), a much-seen symbol at this time of year.

Festive fare varies, but sour cream porridge, traditionally hiding an almond, is a lunchtime favourite inland. *Lutefisk* is most often eaten on the coast, where it is a speciality, usually followed by a whole cod. Roast rib or loin of pork is eaten in central and eastern Norway. On the west coast, the traditional dish is *pinnekjøtt*, smoked and dried lamb ribs.

On Christmas Day there is usually an *koldt bord*, or cold table. A Christmas ham

Above: A small child waits patiently to receive their freshly made Christmas pancake.

studded with cloves provides a festive centrepiece, sometimes given extra flavour by being cured in a beer brine before being smoked. The Christmas baking tradition is still strong, and custom used to dictate that seven different kinds of cookies were baked and offered alongside pancakes and coffee. What's more, no guest can leave without eating as it is said to bring bad luck.

Classic Ingredients

The wild expanses of Norway and its natural supplies of fish, game, dairy products, fruit and vegetables mean that fresh and preserved local foodstuffs form the basis of the cuisine.

Fish and shellfish
One of Norway's most important staple foods has always been fish. Cod is still a crucial mainstay of the diet and economy, with herring rivalling cod in popularity. Other common fish include sprat, haddock, ocean perch and catfish. The seas around Norway also offer a range of shellfish including prawns (shrimp), mussels and Norway lobster, which is smaller and has a brighter pink shell than the American variety.

Norwegian salmon is regarded all over the world as of the highest quality. *Salmo salar*, Atlantic salmon, has long provided great fishing in the favourable Gulf Stream temperatures.

Norway's lakes and rivers also yield a rich harvest of fish, with perch, grayling, bream, arctic char and brown trout inhabiting the clear and bright freshwaters.

Domestic and wild meat
Beef is raised in the southern peninsula and is a frequent sight on the Norwegian table. Sheep and goats are raised in the mountain and fjord areas. In summer, they are taken up to mountain pastures. There they graze on the rich, green grass and develop meat with exceptional flavour. Lamb is often cooked in Norway and forms the basis of many traditional dishes, such as the casserole *fårikål*.

The traditional pastime of hunting has always provided Norwegians with valuable meat protein. Elk (moose) can be found throughout Norway, from the forests in the south right up to the lower part of Finnmark in the north. Norway also has large herds of both wild and domestic reindeer (caribou), as well as deer in the south.

Smaller game also proliferate. Hare (jack rabbit) is found throughout the country, mostly on mountain moors but sometimes in woodland areas, too. Mountain ptarmigan (small grouse) live on high and stony mountainsides, with larger wood ptarmigan in the forests. Black and wood grouse are considered at their most delicious in autumn, when they are plump after feasting all summer on a plentiful diet of berries, which helps to produce their flavoursome flesh.

Below: Salted herrings are an important fish in Norway.

Right: Domestic reindeer grazing near Lake Femunden.

Above: Jarlsberg, Norway's most famous cheese.

Dairy

Norwegians have always valued dairy products with every small farm having at least one cow. Historically, sour milk and cream were an important part of the diet and they are still popular. The daily drink used to be *blande*, sour milk mixed with water, which is still a favourite.

Norway has a rich cheese tradition. The smooth texture of many cheeses makes them easy to slice with a special flat-bladed cutter. Most people associate Norway wth Jarlsberg, a semi-hard cheese with the large holes and pale colour of Emmental, but other Norwegian

cheeses include gräddost, a soft cheese used in open sandwiches; *ridder*, which has a piquant flavour that deepens with age and comes with its distinctive orange outer coating; sveister, with large holes and a rich, sweet, slightly nutty taste; and *nøkkelost*, which includes caraway and cloves, making it slightly acidic.

Vegetables

While the range is not large, vegetables grow well in Norway. Root vegetables such as turnips, parsnips, and swedes (rutabagas) that can be stored for winter are all favourites. Best-loved of all is the potato. Not only is it used as vegetable at almost every meal, potato flour thickens sauces and casseroles and is also mixed with wheat flour for lighter cakes. Cabbage is a much-used vegetable and Norway's pickled version of the German sauerkraut, *surkål*, is so commonplace that ready-prepared versions are bought in large quantities. Cauliflower and broccoli are also well liked.

Above: The humble potato is Norway's national vegetable.

Cereals and beans

The main cereals are barley, oats and rye. Barley is made into porridge, used whole in soups and stews and ground as a flour. It is used to make the traditional Scandinavian flat bread. Dried peas, such as the Scandinavian yellow pea, provide a sustaining base for soups.

Wild produce

The forests of Norway are home to a variety of wild fruit. In summer, there are wild strawberries and raspberries, which are intensely flavoured miniature versions of the cultivated varieties. From mid

July a profusion of berries grow on low bushes: blueberries on open uplands; swamp-loving bilberries; high- and low-bush cranberries; lingonberries and the unparalleled cloudberries. These grow one per stalk and look slightly like an amber-coloured, fat raspberry but have a unique flavour. They are very difficult to find and considerable efforts are made by fruit pickers to protect their location.

In the woods are chanterelle and other wild mushrooms. Norwegians are keen mushroom hunters and there are special checkpoints where the day's harvest are checked for edibility.

Below: Cloudberries are hard to find but taste superb.

Herbs and spices

Norwegians never used to use many flavourings. Salt was the most important seasoning but was used more as a preservative than an intensifier of flavour.

However, certain herbs and spices have become standards for adding flavour. Many, such as parsley, thyme, rosemary and caraway, grow wild. Dill, closely associated with all Scandinavian food, particularly fish, is a member of the parsley family. Juniper trees grow high in the mountains and their berries and young sprigs provide a good alternative to dill for flavouring gravlaks but are also used to add spice to meat.

The two favourite Norwegian spices are cardamom and cinnamon. Cardamom is a useful flavouring for a wide range of baked goods and cinnamon is used in baking and in certain sweet dishes. Caraway is considered to be the oldest cultivated European spice plant and Norwegians value it highly, especially for flavouring the cabbage dish *surkål*.

Bread

Hardbreads were prepared from the autumn grain harvest and were stored for consumption during the winter. Some hardbreads are round with a hole in the middle, enabling them to be threaded on sticks for easy storage. Flat bread, or *flatbrød*, is made with barley flour, salt and water and is eaten with salted meats and soups. Another traditional bread, called *lefse*, was popular among fishermen because it would keep fresh during their trips. When dried out, lefse can be softened by being wrapped in a damp towel for a few hours.

Below: Cinnamon is a best-loved spice in Norway.

Scandinavian Delights

The food in Norway is defined by its simple, delicate flavours and its celebration of fresh local produce, carefully harvested and then lovingly preserved to last throughout the year. From warming winter soups bolstered by barley flour and spiced with juniper berries, to wholesome roast pork loin with pickled red cabbage, the good husbandry practices and creativity of Norwegian cooks through the ages is still present today. This collection of recipes celebrates the very best of Norwegian cuisine such as simple dishes from the *koldt bord* or elaborate confections filled with cream and wild berries.

Left: Fresh fish and shellfish feature on every Norwegian koldt table.

Herrings with Carrot and Leek
Spekesild med Gulrötter

Serves 4 as an appetizer

2 salt herring fillets or 2 jars
   (150–200g/5–7oz) herring fillets
   in brine, drained (these do not
   need soaking)
200ml/7fl oz/¾ cup water
400ml/14fl oz/1½ cups wine vinegar
150g/5oz/¾ cup sugar
1 onion, finely sliced
1 bay leaf
6 whole allspice
6 whole peppercorns
1 small carrot, finely sliced
½ small leek, white part only, finely
   sliced
2 shallots, quartered

*Marinated herrings can be
dressed in a number of
different ways. Here, they
are combined with finely
carrots and leeks for a
tasty appetizer.*

1 Soak the herring fillets in cold water for 8–12 hours. Drain, rinse under cold water and place in a glass jar.

2 Put the water, vinegar and sugar in a large bowl and stir until the sugar has dissolved. Add the onion, bay leaf, allspice and peppercorns then pour over the herring fillets. Leave in a cold place for 6–12 hours.

3 Cut the herring fillets into 2.5cm/1in thick pieces then arrange the pieces on a serving dish as if they were still whole.

4 Add a little of the marinade to the fillets and then the sliced carrot and leek. Place the quartered shallots around the edge of the dish and serve.

Salted Herrings in Sherry
Sherrysild

Serves 4 as an appetizer

2–3 matjes herrings
60ml/4 tbsp water
100ml/3½fl oz/scant ½ cup
 medium-dry sherry
30ml/2 tbsp wine vinegar
45ml/3 tbsp sugar
1 onion, finely sliced
5 peppercorns, crushed
fresh dill fronds, to garnish

1 The matjes herrings will not need pre-marinating. Cut the herrings into 2.5cm/1in pieces and arrange on a serving dish. Put the water, sherry and vinegar in a large bowl, add the sugar and stir until dissolved.

2 Pour the dressing over the herrings. Arrange the sliced onion on top and sprinkle with the crushed peppercorns. Leave to marinate in a cold place for 2–3 hours. Serve garnished with dill fronds.

This recipe uses matjes herrings rather than pre-marinated ones. Here, the marinade is formed of water, sherry, vinegar and sugar – easy to prepare and wonderful to eat.

Serves 3–4

500g/1¼lb middle cut of salmon,
    or fat trout, mackerel or herring
    fillets, with skin on
25g/1oz/2 tbsp crushed sea salt
25–50g/1–2oz/2–4 tbsp sugar
5ml/1 tsp crushed white peppercorns
15ml/1 tbsp chopped fresh juniper
    sprigs or dill, plus extra to garnish
15ml/1 tbsp Cognac
lemon wedges, to garnish

For the mustard sauce

1 egg yolk
15ml/1 tbsp sweet Scandinavian
    mustard, or substitute with French
    mustard
15ml/1 tbsp sugar
150ml/¼ pint/⅔ cup light olive oil
15ml/1 tbsp white wine vinegar
15–30ml/1–2 tbsp chopped juniper
    sprigs or 30–45ml/2–3 tbsp
    chopped fresh dill
salt and ground black pepper

Marinated Salmon Gravlaks

1 Scrape the scales off the fish. Leave the skin on as it makes the fish easier to slice after marinating. Wipe the fish with damp kitchen paper.

2 Mix together the salt, sugar and the peppercorns. Using a shallow dish, line with a piece of foil large enough to wrap the fish in, and a layer of juniper or dill. Place one piece of fish, skin side down, on the juniper or dill. Rub one third of the salt mixture into the flesh and add a layer of juniper or dill. Rub another third of the salt into the flesh of the second piece of fish and place on the first, matching thinner side to thicker so that the fish makes as even a parcel as possible. Rub the last third of salt mixture into the top skin and add the remaining juniper or dill.

3 Sprinkle the Cognac over the fish. Cover with the foil, place a small board on top and weight the fish down. Leave in a cool pantry or refrigerator for 36–48 hours, depending on the thickness of the fish.

4 For the sauce, use all ingredients at room temperature. Mix the egg yolk, mustard and sugar together and drizzle the oil into the mixture, whisking to form a thick, shiny sauce. Whisk in the vinegar and add the juniper or dill and season.

5 Scrape all the seasonings off the marinated fish and remove any bones. Slice the fish (thick slices are traditional), from one end, at 45 degrees. Serve garnished with lemon wedges and dill and accompany with the mustard sauce.

It was the Swedes who first made salmon marinated with dill popular, but Norway, with its plentiful supply of salmon, wasn't far behind. Norwegians marinate the fish with dill but also use juniper sprigs as an alternative. Trout, herring and mackerel can be marinated in the same way as salmon. It is best served simply on thin slices of rye bread.

Serves 6–8
butter, for greasing
250g/9oz hard back pork fat, thinly
    sliced
500g/1¼lb pig's liver
1 onion, chopped
5 anchovy fillets
60ml/4 tbsp plain (all-purpose) flour
100ml/3½fl oz/scant ½ cup milk
100ml/3½fl oz/scant ½ cup double
    (heavy) cream
2 large eggs
1.5ml/¼ tsp ground cloves
1.5ml/¼ tsp ground allspice
pinch of cayenne pepper
115g/4oz/1⅔ cup mushrooms,
    chopped and sautéed in butter
    (optional)
salt and ground black pepper

Liver Pâté Leverpostei

1 Preheat the oven to 180°C/350°F/Gas 4. Generously butter a 1kg/2¼lb loaf tin (pan). Line the bottom of the tin, using about a third of the sliced pork fat.

2 Cut the pig's liver and the remaining pork fat into small pieces and mince (grind) with the onion and anchovy fillets. For the best results, the mixture should be put through a mincer (grinder) at least three times and five is better. Alternatively, use a blender or food processor to mince the ingredients together. If using a blender or food processor, then push the mixture through a sieve (strainer) after mincing because these machines tend to leave odd strings of membrane. This process sounds hard work, but it does ensure a really smooth pâté. Only mincing once or using a blender or processor without straining will produce a coarser result but the flavour should still be excellent.

3 Add the flour, milk, cream, eggs, cloves, allspice, cayenne pepper and mushrooms, if using, to the mixture and season with salt and pepper. Mix well together and pour into the prepared loaf tin.

4 Cover the loaf tin with buttered foil, place in a roasting pan and fill with hot water to come about two-thirds of the way up the sides of the pan. Bake in the oven for about 1 hour, until the tip of a sharp knife, inserted in the centre, comes out clean. Leave the pâté to cool in the tin before serving with green salad leaves.

Traditionally, every Norwegian cook had their favourite pâté recipe. The majority are made with pig's liver, as in this version, which is simple to prepare, and best eaten a couple of days after cooking to allow its flavours to develop fully.

Wild Mushroom Soup Soppsuppe

1 If using the dried mushrooms, put in a small bowl and pour over a generous amount of boiling water. Leave to soak for at least 20 minutes, until the mushrooms are soft. Using a slotted spoon, remove the mushrooms from the bowl then strain the soaking liquid and reserve. Chop the dried mushrooms.

2 Put the sliced fresh mushrooms in a pan, cover with the stock and simmer for 10 minutes. Strain the stock and reserve.

3 Melt the butter in a large pan, add the sliced fresh mushrooms and the soaked dried mushrooms (if using) and fry gently for 2–3 minutes, then season with salt and pepper.

4 Stir the flour into the pan and cook over a low heat for 1–2 minutes, without colouring. Remove from the heat and gradually stir in the reserved stock and the dried mushroom soaking liquid to form a smooth sauce. Return to the heat and, stirring all the time, cook until the sauce boils and thickens. Lower the heat and simmer gently for 5–10 minutes.

5 Add the cream to the soup then add lemon juice to taste. Finally, add the sherry, if using. Pour the soup into individual warmed serving bowls and top with a little cream swirled on top of each and a final garnish of chopped parsley.

A large proportion of Norway is forested and wild mushrooms are plentiful. Norwegians are skilled at knowing which ones are edible and which ones should be avoided. Late summer and autumn are the best times to go mushroom hunting. One way of using the abundant harvest is in this nourishing soup.

Serves 4

10g/¼oz/1 tbsp dried mushrooms, such as ceps (optional), if fresh wild mushrooms are unavailable

400g/14oz fresh mushrooms, preferably wild, sliced

1.25 litres/2¼ pints/5½ cups light stock, vegetable or chicken

50g/2oz/4 tbsp butter

30–45ml/2–3 tbsp plain (all-purpose) white flour

60ml/4 tbsp double (heavy) cream, plus extra to garnish

a squeeze of fresh lemon juice

15–30ml/1–2 tbsp medium sherry (optional)

salt and ground black pepper

chopped fresh parsley, to garnish

Apple and Juniper Soup Eplesuppe med enerbær

Serves 4

15ml/1 tbsp juniper berries
4 cardamom pods
3 whole allspice
1 small cinnamon stick
bunch of fresh parsley
30ml/2 tbsp olive oil
3 cooking apples, peeled, cored and diced
2 celery sticks, finely chopped
2 shallots, chopped
2.5cm/1in piece fresh root ginger, finely chopped
1 litre/1¾ pints/4 cups light chicken stock
250ml/8fl oz/1 cup cider
250ml/8fl oz/1 cup double (heavy) cream
75ml/5 tbsp Armagnac (optional)
salt and ground black pepper
chopped fresh parsley, to garnish

This is an example of the savoury fruit soups that are popular throughout northern Europe. The apple and juniper berry flavours are particularly Norwegian.

1 Put the juniper berries, cardamom pods, allspice and cinnamon stick in a piece of muslin (cheesecloth) and tie together with string. Tie the parsley together.

2 Heat the oil in a pan, add the apples, celery, shallots and ginger, and season with salt and pepper. Place a piece of dampened baking parchment on top, cover the pan and cook gently for 10 minutes. Discard the parchment.

3 Add the stock and cider and stir well. Add the spices and parsley. Bring slowly to the boil, then lower the heat and simmer for 40 minutes. Remove the spices and parsley.

4 Pour the soup into a blender and blend until smooth. Then pass it through a sieve (strainer) into a clean pan. Bring to the boil and add the cream and Armagnac, if using. Add salt and pepper if necessary. Serve hot, garnished with parsley.

Curry Soup Karrisuppe

Serves 4

50g/2oz/4 tbsp butter
2 shallots, finely chopped
1 cooking apple, peeled, cored and
    chopped
10ml/2 tsp curry paste
30ml/2 tbsp plain (all-purpose) flour
1.25 litres/2¼ pints/5½ cups
    chicken or beef stock
400ml/14fl oz can unsweetened
    coconut milk
salt and ground black pepper
60ml/4 tbsp double (heavy) cream
    or 4 tbsp of the coconut milk and
    chopped fresh parsley, to garnish

Indian spices have been enjoyed in Norway for centuries, particularly in the south of the country, and curry powder enlivens many dishes. More recently, South-east Asian food has become popular and the coconut milk here replaces the more usual cream.

1 Melt the butter in a pan, add the shallots and cook gently for about 5 minutes until softened but not coloured. Add the apple, season with salt and pepper and cook for another 2 minutes, until the apple is slightly softened.

2 Stir the curry paste and flour into the pan and cook over a low heat for 1–2 minutes, without colouring. Remove from the heat and gradually stir in the stock to form a smooth sauce. Return to the heat and, stirring all the time, cook until the sauce boils and thickens. Lower the heat and simmer gently for 10 minutes.

3 Add the coconut milk to the soup and stir well. Check the seasonings, adding salt and pepper if necessary. Pour the soup into individual serving bowls and serve with a swirl of cream or coconut milk on top of each and chopped parsley, to garnish.

Salmon Rolls with Asparagus and Butter Sauce
Lakserulader med asparges

Serves 4
4 thick or 8 thin asparagus spears
4 very thin slices salmon fillet, each
   weighing about 115g/4oz
juice 1 lemon
salt and ground black pepper

For the butter sauce
1 shallot, finely chopped
6 peppercorns
120ml/4fl oz/½ cup dry white wine
60ml/4 tbsp double (heavy) cream
200g/7oz/scant 1 cup butter, cut into
   small cubes
1 bunch fresh parsley, chopped,
   to serve
salt and ground black pepper

1 Steam the asparagus spears for 6–8 minutes, according to their size, until tender. Refresh under cold running water, drain and set aside.

2 The slices of salmon should be wide enough to roll around the asparagus. Don't worry if they have to be patched together. Place the slices on a surface, season with salt and pepper, lay one or two asparagus spears across each slice and then roll the salmon around them. Place the rolls on a rack over a pan of boiling water, sprinkle with lemon juice, and cover and steam for 3–4 minutes until tender.

3 To make the butter sauce, put the shallot, peppercorns and wine in a small pan and heat gently until the wine has reduced to a tablespoonful. Strain and return to the pan. Add the cream, bring to the boil, and then lower the heat.

4 Add the butter to the sauce in small pieces, whisking all the time until well incorporated before adding another piece. Do not allow the sauce to boil or it will separate. Season the sauce with salt and pepper to taste, if necessary. If you wish, the sauce can be kept warm by putting it in a bowl, standing over a pan of gently simmering water.

5 Add the chopped parsley to the sauce and serve with the salmon rolls on warmed plates.

Asparagus has been a popular ingredient in Norway for many years and its green spears appear each year as a welcome sign of spring. In this recipe, the green contrasts beautifully with the pink flesh of the salmon and each has a sweetness of flavour that marries perfectly.

Serves 4

50g/2oz/½ cup plain (all-purpose) flour

675g/1½lb pollock fillet, skinned and cut into 4 serving portions

50g/2oz/4 tbsp butter

15ml/1 tbsp vegetable oil

2 large onions, sliced

5ml/1 tsp sugar

200ml/7fl oz/scant 1 cup water

salt and ground black pepper

Pollock with Onions
Lyr med løk

1 Preheat the oven to 180°C/350°F/Gas 4. Put the flour on a large plate and season with salt and pepper. Dip the fish portions in the flour to coat on both sides. Put a knob of the butter and the oil in a large frying pan and heat until the butter has melted. Add the floured fish and fry quickly on both sides until browned. Place in an ovenproof dish.

2 Melt the remaining butter in the same pan, add the onions, season with salt and pepper and fry gently for about 10 minutes until softened and golden brown. Add the sugar, increase the heat and allow the onion to caramelize slightly.

3 Spread the onions over the fish. Add the water to the frying pan, stirring to lift any sediment on the bottom of the pan, bring to the boil then pour over the fish and onions. Bake in the oven for about 20 minutes, until the fish is tender.

4 Serve with boiled potatoes and a green vegetable.

Pollock is a favourite, less expensive alternative to cod and it is often served along the Norwegian coast. The flesh is much firmer than cod and has a slighlty pearly hue. It is full of flavour and forms a delicious partnership with the fried onions that feature in this dish.

Shellfish Salad Skalldyrsalat

Serves 4

115g/4oz/1¾ cups mushrooms,
  sliced
juice ½ lemon
1 lobster, about 450g/1lb, cooked
  and with meat extracted
115g/4oz/1 cup cooked fresh or
  canned asparagus
1 crisp lettuce, shredded
16 cooked mussels
115g/4oz/½ cup cooked peeled
  prawns (shrimp)
2 tomatoes, skinned and quartered
dill fronds, to garnish

For the dressing

30ml/2 tbsp white wine vinegar
90–120ml/6–8 tbsp olive oil
pinch of sugar
salt and ground black pepper

This salad appears on all Norwegian cold tables for special occasions, with the shellfish chosen according to its availability and taste. When fresh shellfish is scarce, frozen or canned is an alternative.

1 Chill all the salad ingredients in the refrigerator before use. To make the dressing, put the vinegar, oil, and sugar in a bowl and mix well together. Season the dressing with salt and pepper to taste.

2 Put the mushrooms in a serving bowl and sprinkle over the lemon juice. Cut the lobster meat into bitesize pieces and add to the bowl. Cut the fresh or canned asparagus into 5cm/2in pieces and add to the bowl. Add the lettuce in a layer, the mussels, prawns and tomatoes.

3 Pour the dressing over the salad ingredients and toss together. Garnish with dill fronds and serve immediately.

Crisp Fried Herrings Sprøstekt sild

Serves 4

4 herrings, filleted

50g/2oz/⅓ cup plain (all-purpose)
    flour

1 egg

115g/4oz/2 cups fine dried
    breadcrumbs

40g/1½oz/3 tbsp butter

salt and ground black pepper

1 Rinse the herring fillets under cold water and dry on kitchen paper. Put the flour on a plate and season with salt and pepper. Break the egg in a bowl and beat lightly. Spread the breadcrumbs on another plate. Dip the fish fillets in the flour, to coat on both sides, then into the beaten egg and then the breadcrumbs.

2 Melt the butter in a large frying pan, add the coated fillets and fry over a medium heat for about 3–4 minutes on each side, until golden brown.

3 Serve with mustard sauce (see page 20) or sour cream and pickled beetroot (beet), boiled potatoes and a green vegetable.

Herrings are an integral part of Norwegian cuisine. Salted herrings are essential on any Norwegian cold table and fresh herrings, crisply fried as in this recipe, are a welcome feature of any family meal.

Salted Cod Casserole Bacalao

Serves 4

1kg/2¼lb salt cod
about 500g/1¼lb potatoes, sliced
1 onion, sliced
100ml/3½fl oz/scant ½ cup water
100ml/3½fl oz/scant ½ cup olive oil
75ml/2½fl oz/⅓ cup strained canned
   tomatoes
a little chopped red chilli

1 Soak the cod in cold water for 2 days, changing the water at least 3 times a day. Drain and remove the skin and bones, then cut the fish into pieces measuring about 5cm/2in square.

2 Layer the fish, potatoes and finally the onion in a medium flameproof casserole. Put the water, oil, strained tomatoes and the chilli in a pan and bring to the boil. Pour into the casserole.

3 Return the liquid to the boil, reduce the heat, cover and simmer for 1½–2 hours, until the potatoes are tender.

COOK'S TIP

It helps to have two sharp knives for preparing the cod: a small one to cut away the flesh from the bones, and a larger, flexible-bladed one to slide, in a sawing motion, between the flesh and the skin. A little salt on the fingers will help to grip the skin.

Bacalao is a type of dried and salted fish used in Portugal and Spain, but in Norway it means a casserole made from salt cod, tomatoes, potatoes and oil. This dish is a particular favourite in the salt-fish ports of Kristiansund and Alesund.

Beef Meatballs in Gravy
Kjøttkaker med kålstuing

1 Put the minced beef in a bowl and add the grated nutmeg, ground allspice, ground ginger, potato flour, and 5ml/1 tsp salt and pepper, and beat well. Add the milk or water, little by little, beating after each addition. Add the beaten egg and beat well again.

2 With wet hands, shape the mixture into balls (the balls can be any size you like but the larger the balls, the longer it will take to cook them).

3 Heat the oil in a large frying pan, add the meatballs and fry over a medium heat until cooked. If necessary, fry them in batches. Remove them and transfer to a plate.

4 When the meatballs are cooked, add the butter and heat until melted. Add the flour, stirring to deglaze the pan, scraping up any sediment. Gradually add the stock, stirring all the time to form a smooth sauce. When all the stock has been added, bring slowly to the boil, stirring, until the sauce boils and thickens. Check the seasonings, adding salt and pepper only if necessary, then simmer for 10 minutes.

5 Add the cream to the sauce, then add the meatballs and simmer for a further 10 minutes. Serve hot.

Serves 4

500g/1¼lb finely minced (ground) beef
large pinch of grated nutmeg
large pinch of ground allspice
large pinch of ground ginger
15ml/1 tbsp potato flour
200ml/7fl oz/scant 1 cup milk or water
1 egg, lightly beaten
30ml/2 tbsp vegetable oil
25g/1oz/2 tbsp butter
25g/1oz plain (all-purpose) flour
600ml/1 pint/2½ cups beef stock
30–45ml/2–3 tbsp double (heavy) cream
salt and ground black pepper

This is the Norwegian version of meatballs, although everyone in Scandinavia has their own recipe. Traditionally made with beef, some cooks will use a mixture of beef and pork, while others will add finely chopped onions or vary the seasonings.

Lamb and Cabbage Fårikål

Serves 4

1.5kg/3¼lb cabbage, cored and cut into large wedges

675g/1½lb boneless lamb such as shoulder, fillet or lean breast, cut into large pieces

15–30ml/1–2 tbsp plain (all-purpose) flour (optional)

salt

15ml/1 tbsp black peppercorns

300–450ml/½–¾ pint/1¼–scant 2 cups boiling water

This casserole is almost a national dish. A Fårikål Day is celebrated in the autumn and the dish is loved by every Norwegian. It doesn't matter which cut of lamb is used; the combination of sweet lamb and cabbage is comforting and delicious. The peppercorns yield their fierceness in the cooking and add a pleasant punch to the taste.

1 Using a large flameproof casserole and starting with the cabbage, put the cabbage and lamb in layers, sprinkling each of the layers with flour, if using, salt and peppercorns.

2 Pour over enough boiling water to cover both the cabbage and lamb. Bring the casserole to the boil, and then reduce the heat and simmer over a low heat for about 1½ hours, until the meat is tender. Serve very hot on warmed plates, accompanied with boiled potatoes.

VARIATION

Using stock instead of water adds flavour and, for additional taste, some cooks include caraway seeds with the peppercorns.

Fried Pork and Apples Epleflesk

Serves 4

600g/1lb 6oz lightly salted or fresh
    belly of pork, cut into thin slices
500g/1¼lb crisp eating apples
30ml/2 tbsp soft light brown sugar
salt and ground black pepper
chopped fresh parsley, to garnish

This is a very simple dish that turns an inexpensive cut of meat into a most enjoyable meal. It is ideal for a quick supper dish. Norwegian apples are very crisp and have a beautiful flavour; the summer may not be long but the days are filled with almost 24 hours of sunshine, which helps the fruit to ripen.

1 Heat a large frying pan, without any oil or fat, until hot. Add the pork slices and fry over a low heat, 3–4 minutes each side, until golden brown. Season the pork slices with salt and pepper. Transfer to a warmed serving dish and keep warm.

2 Core the apples but do not peel, then cut the apples into rings to a depth of 5mm/¼in across the apple. Add the apple rings to the frying pan and fry gently in the pork fat, 3–4 minutes each side, until just beginning to turn golden and translucent. Sprinkle the slices with the sugar and turn once more for a couple of minutes until the sugar side starts to caramelize.

3 Serve the pork slices with the apple rings. Accompany with boiled potatoes and a green vegetable, garnished with chopped parsley.

Roast Pork Loin with Red Cabbage
Svinestek med rødkål

Serves 6–8

2kg/4½lb pork loin, rind scored into
    2.5cm/1in squares
500ml/17fl oz/generous 2 cups
    water
salt and ground black pepper

For the red cabbage

25g/1oz/2 tbsp butter
1 red cabbage, total weight about
    1.2kg/2½lb, cored and finely
    sliced
2 cooking apples, peeled, cored and
    diced
15ml/1 tbsp caraway seeds (optional)
90ml/6 tbsp cider vinegar
150ml/¼ pint/⅔ cup water
60ml/4 tbsp rowan or redcurrant jelly
30–45ml/2–3 tbsp sugar
salt and ground black pepper

1 To prepare the pork, rub the pork rind with salt and pepper. Put in the refrigerator and leave for 24 hours or even a little longer.

2 To prepare the red cabbage, melt the butter in a large flameproof casserole or pan. Add the shredded cabbage, apples and caraway seeds, if using, salt and pepper and fry gently, tossing the ingredients together until well mixed and coated in butter. Take care not to allow the cabbage to catch on the bottom of the pan.

3 Add the vinegar and water to the pan, cover and cook gently for 2 hours until the cabbage is tender. Add the jelly and sugar to taste. The cabbage is better if allowed to cool, kept in the refrigerator overnight and reheated the following day.

4 When ready to cook the pork, preheat the oven to 240°C/475°F/Gas 9. Put the loin, rind side down, in a roasting pan and add the water. Cover with foil and put in the oven for 20 minutes.

5 Reduce the oven temperature to 180°C/350°F/Gas 4. Remove the foil, turn the meat rind side up, and roast for 1½ hours. Increase the heat to 230°C/450°F/Gas 8 and roast for a further 20 minutes, until the crackling is crisp.

6 Meanwhile, turn the red cabbage into a large pan. Some 20 minutes before serving, gently reheat the cabbage. Serve the pork with the red cabbage, and accompany with roast potatoes and a green salad.

A roast pork loin, served with red cabbage, is a Norwegian Christmas festive dish. The rind of the pork is scored into squares and there is much competition amongst Norwegian cooks to achieve a really crisp crackling.

Braised Chicken with Mashed Swede
Stekt kylling med kålrotstuing

1 Put 50g/2oz/4 tbsp of the butter, parsley, salt and pepper inside the chicken. Heat the oil and the rest of the butter in a flameproof casserole. Add the chicken and brown on all sides. Season.

2 Lower the heat, cover the pan and simmer gently for 1 hour. Test by inserting the point of a sharp knife into the thigh near the body until the juices are clear.

3 Prepare the mashed swede. Put the swede in a large pan, cover with water and season with salt. Bring to the boil, lower the heat and simmer for 15 minutes.

4 Add the potatoes to the pan of swedes and simmer for 15 minutes. Drain, reserving a little water, and return the vegetables to the pan. Mash well, then add the butter and allspice. Season the mashed vegetables with salt and pepper.

5 When cooked, transfer the chicken to a warmed serving dish. Add a little water to the pan to make a simple gravy, stirring to deglaze the pan and scraping up any sediment from the bottom. Serve the chicken with the gravy and mashed swede.

Serves 4
75g/3oz/6 tbsp butter
1 small bunch fresh parsley
1.6kg/3½lb chicken
15ml/1 tbsp vegetable oil
salt and ground black pepper

For the mashed swede (rutabaga)
450g/1lb swedes (rutabaga), cut into
  cubes
675g/1½lb potatoes, cut into cubes
about 115g/4oz/½ cup butter
pinch of ground allspice
salt and ground black pepper

This traditional way of cooking chicken maintains maximum flavour and produces delicious juices in the dish. It is served with a mixture of mashed swede and potato, both absorbing the butter to give a creamy purée.

Reindeer Terrine with Juniper Berries and Aquavit Rådyrpostei med enerbær og akevitt

Serves 6–8

500g/1¼lb reindeer or stewing venison, finely chopped

500g/1¼lb fat belly of pork, minced (ground)

10ml/2 tsp chopped fresh thyme

10ml/2 tsp chopped fresh rosemary

6 juniper berries, well crushed

a little grated nutmeg

50ml/2fl oz/¼ cup aquavit or brandy

1 garlic clove

10ml/2 tsp sea salt

1 bay leaf

6–8 slices unsmoked streaky (fatty) bacon, rind removed

200ml/7fl oz/scant 1 cup double (heavy) cream

ground black pepper

1 Put the meat, herbs, juniper berries, nutmeg, pepper and aquavit or brandy in a bowl. Crush the garlic with the salt and add to the mixture. Cover and leave in the refrigerator overnight or for at least 8 hours.

2 The next day, preheat the oven to150°C/300°F/Gas 2. Put the bay leaf in the bottom of a 1kg/2¼lb loaf tin (pan). With the back of a knife, stretch the streaky bacon and line the tin.

3 Add the cream to the meat mixture and mix in well. Turn the mixture into the tin and flip the ends of the bacon slices over the mixture. Place the tin in a roasting pan and fill with hot water to come halfway up the sides of the pan. Bake the terrine in the oven for about 1½ hours or until the terrine starts to come away from the sides of the tin.

4 Remove the tin from the oven and put on a heatproof tray, dish or pan with sides. Place a board on top and weight it down so the juices overflow. Leave the terrine to cool then remove from the tin, wrap in foil and chill in the refrigerator before serving.

This simple stewing venison recipe makes a hearty terrine. It is full of flavour, and is ideal for a summer picnic or a cold table. Preparation starts a day before cooking and the terrine is best eaten 2 to 3 days after making it to allow its flavours to mature.

Roe Deer Medallions with Redcurrants
Rådyrmedaljonger med rips

1 Preheat the oven to 200°C/400°F/Gas 6. Season the venison medallions with salt and pepper. Heat the butter and oil in a large frying pan, add the medallions and quickly sear on both sides, then put on a baking tray and set aside.

2 Add the stock to the pan, stirring to deglaze and scraping up any sediment from the bottom of the pan. Add the port and cream, stir well together, then cook until reduced by half. Season the sauce with salt and pepper to taste. Add the redcurrants and a knob of butter.

3 Roast the medallions in the oven for 4–5 minutes, according to size, until slightly underdone. Place the medallions on individual warmed serving plates or a serving dish, pour a little sauce over each and serve the remaining sauce separately. Accompany with boiled new potatoes, glazed onions and a green salad.

COOK'S TIP

The meat needs to be served slightly underdone, which means the roasted medallions should give a little when pressed.

This is a dish that should be cooked for a special occasion. The equivalent cut of beef would be tournedos from the fillet. With venison or roe deer the fillet is much smaller, so ask for the medallions to be cut from the thick end of the fillet and allow two per person.

Serves 4

about 800g/1¾lb venison fillet,
    preferably roe deer, cut into 8
    medallions
15g/½oz/1 tbsp butter
15ml/1 tbsp vegetable oil
salt and ground black pepper

For the sauce

200ml/7fl oz/scant 1 cup venison or
    beef stock
150ml/5fl oz/⅔ cup port
100ml/3½fl oz/scant ½ cup double
    (heavy) cream
30ml/2 tbsp redcurrants
a knob of butter

Pheasant Stuffed with Mountain Fruits
Farsert orrfuglstek i gryte

Serves 6–8

1.8–2.25kg/4–5lb pheasant or black
   grouse, plucked and drawn
15g/½oz/1 tbsp unsalted butter
75ml/2½fl oz/⅓ cup medium white
   wine
1 rosemary sprig
100ml/3½fl oz/scant ½ cup sour
   cream or crème fraîche
salt and ground black pepper

For the stuffing

115g/4oz/½ cup pitted prunes
2 apples
juice 1 lemon
115g/4oz/1 cup fresh blueberries or
   dried cranberries
5ml/1 tsp chopped fresh rosemary
salt and ground black pepper

*The lean, tender meat of
the pheasant has always
been a great European
delicacy. The sweetness
of the fruit stuffing balances
the bird's gamey flavour.*

1 Cut the prunes into small pieces and put in a bowl. Peel, core and finely dice the apples and add to the prunes. Pour over the lemon juice. Add the berries and rosemary, season and mix together. Fill the bird with the stuffing and truss with string (see cook's tip).

2 Melt the butter in a flameproof casserole, and fry the bird until browned. Stand the bird on a small rack in the casserole. Add the wine to cover the rack, and add the rosemary.

3 Cover the casserole and simmer gently for about 1 hour. Insert the point of a sharp knife into the thigh near the body – if the juices are clear, the bird is cooked. Remove the bird and rack from the casserole, put on a warmed serving dish and keep warm.

4 Discard the rosemary sprig and add the sour cream or crème fraîche to the pan juices. Heat the juices, stirring well, until the sauce is a good pouring consistency.

5 Carve the bird, arrange on a dish and garnish with the stuffing and a little sauce. Accompany with the remaining sauce, boiled potatoes and a green vegetable or salad.

COOK'S TIP

Trussing a chicken involves tying kitchen twine around the wings and legs so that they stay close to the body and ensures that the bird cooks evenly. Start with 1m/3ft of kitchen twine. Position the chicken breast-side up with the legs facing you and place the centre of the twine under the tailbone. Lift the twine, loop each end around the legs and reverse the twine to make a cross. Pull tightly so that the legs come together. Next, pull the twine around the front of the chicken and over the wings. Flip the chicken upside down so that the neck is now facing you and tie a knot underneath the neckbone.

Norwegian Pancakes
Pannekaker

1 Melt the butter. Put the eggs in a bowl and beat lightly together, then sift in the flour. Add the milk, melted butter, salt and cinnamon and mix together to form a smooth, thin batter. Alternatively, this can be done in a food processor. Leave to rest in a cool place for 30 minutes to an hour until the flour is absorbed into the mixture.

2 Heat a frying pan measuring about 18cm/7in. Add a little oil and when hot, add enough batter to swirl around the base of the pan in a thin layer. Cook until golden brown then slip a metal spatula underneath and turn over or toss. Cook briefly on the other side until a spotted brown colour, then remove from the pan and repeat the process with the remaining batter.

3 To serve the pancakes, spread a line of butter across the centre of the pancake, and add jam or sugar and cinnamon. Alternatively, add fresh berries and sour cream or whipped cream, roll up or fold over the pancake and dust with icing sugar.

COOK'S TIP
When turning a pancake over, don't try to flip it in the pan too soon. The secret is to make sure it is cooked before turning.

Serves 12
25g/1oz/2 tbsp butter
3 eggs
115g/4oz/1 cup plain white (all-
    purpose) flour
350ml/12fl oz/1½ cups milk
pinch of salt
pinch of ground cinnamon
vegetable oil, for shallow frying
butter, jam or sugar and cinnamon,
    or fresh fruit berries, such
    as raspberries, sour cream
    or whipped cream and icing
    (confectioners') sugar, to serve

Norwegian pancakes are closely related to French crêpes. They are served with sugar and cinnamon for breakfast, or for dessert filled with lingonberries or strawberries and cream, or a spoonful of blueberry jelly and sour cream.

Rhubarb Soup Rabarbrasuppe

Serves 4

1.2 litre/2 pints/5 cups water
500g/1¼lb rhubarb, cut into small
  lengths
1 cinnamon stick (optional)
150g/5oz/¾ cup sugar
25g/1oz potato flour
pinch of salt
crème fraîche or sour cream, to serve

Traditionally, everyone in Norway had a rhubarb patch, usually near the barn. Rhubarb is a plant that produces ample fruit without taking up much space, which is important when fertile land is limited. Although Norwegians are fond of savoury fruit soups, this is a dessert, made with the first picked rhubarb, and was a traditional treat after the long winter.

1 In a pan, bring the water to the boil. Add the rhubarb and cinnamon stick and simmer for about 5 minutes, until the rhubarb is tender. Remove the cinnamon stick and add sugar to taste.

2 Put the potato flour in a small bowl, add a little water and blend together to form a smooth paste. Add to the rhubarb and heat, stirring all the time, until thickened and clear, but do not bring to the boil. Remove from the heat and add the salt.

3 Serve the soup hot or cold and garnish each bowl with a spoonful of crème fraîche or sour cream.

VARIATIONS

• Add strawberries to the soup, which combine beautifully with the rhubarb.
• Instead of the cinnamon stick, add the grated rind of 1 orange.

Peasant Girls in a Veil Tilslørte Bondepiker

Serves 4

1kg/2¼lb cooking apples
45ml/3 tbsp water
50g/2oz caster (superfine) sugar
115g/4oz/½ cup butter
65g/2½oz/1¼ cups fresh
   breadcrumbs
350ml/12fl oz/1½ cups whipping
   cream
50g/2oz/½ cup toasted almonds,
   roughly chopped, to decorate

1 Peel, core and cut the apples into small pieces. Simmer in a pan with the water for 10–15 minutes until the apples are soft. Leave to cool and add a little sugar to taste.

2 Melt the butter in a frying pan and when hot, add the fresh breadcrumbs and 40g/1½oz sugar and gently fry, stirring frequently, until the breadcrumbs are golden brown. Remove from the heat and leave to cool. (The crumbs will become crisper as they cool.)

3 Whisk the cream until it holds its shape. Layer the apples, cream and breadcrumbs in glass serving dishes, ending with a layer of cream. Sprinkle with the chopped almonds.

COOK'S TIP
Do not prepare the dish too far ahead of serving or the breadcrumbs will lose their crispness.

This cooking apple recipe is probably the most famous Norwegian dessert and is traditional in all the Scandinavian countries. The Norwegian version uses cream in generous layers between the apple sauce and the crumbs. The final layer of cream is the veil in the recipe title.

Caramel Pudding
Karamellpudding

1 Preheat the oven to 160°C/325°F/Gas 3. For the caramel, put 115g/4oz/½ cup sugar in a pan over a medium heat until golden. Add the hot water carefully – standing clear as the sugar can splutter when hot water is added. Stir together. Pour the caramel into a round, 1 litre/¾ pint ovenproof dish and swirl the caramel around to coat the bottom and a little way up the sides. It will set instantly.

2 Mix the eggs and egg yolks and the remaining 30ml/2 tbsp sugar in a bowl (don't whisk). Using the caramel pan, heat the milk with the split vanilla pod to just below boiling.

3 Remove the vanilla pod from the milk and whisk the milk into the egg and sugar. Strain through a sieve (strainer) into the caramel dish. Place in a roasting pan and fill with cold water to come about three-quarters of the way up the sides.

4 Bake the custard for 45 minutes to 1 hour. Leave until cool, then chill for 2–3 hours. Having run a knife around the edge, place a serving dish over the top of the custard and invert the caramel on to the dish. Decorate with chopped almonds.

COOK'S TIP
The creamy texture of the custard depends on slow cooking. Part-filling the roasting pan with cold water helps to filter the heat.

Serves 4

115g/4oz/½ cup plus 30ml/2 tbsp
    caster (superfine) sugar
30ml/2 tbsp hot water
3 large eggs
3 large egg yolks
600ml/20fl oz/2½ cups full fat milk,
    or a mixture of milk and single
    (light) cream
1 vanilla pod (bean), split lengthways
chopped blanched almonds, to
    decorate

Every country home used to have at least one cow, and milk is a staple of the country's diet. This simple but delicious pudding is a great Norwegian favourite.

Cream Layer Cake Bløtkake

1 Preheat the oven to 160°C/325°F/Gas 3. Line a 23cm/9in round cake tin (pan) with baking parchment. Sift the flour and baking powder together. Put the eggs and sugar in a bowl and whisk until pale and the mixture will form ribbons on the surface if lifted and allowed to fall back into the bowl. Fold in the sifted flour until well combined. Turn the mixture into the prepared tin.

2 Bake the cake in the oven for about 40 minutes until firm to the touch and beginning to come away from the sides of the tin. Leave in the tin for 5 minutes, then carefully turn out on to a wire rack to cool.

3 Meanwhile whip the whipping cream until it holds its shape.

4 Cut the cooled cake horizontally into three rounds. Place the top round, upside down, on to a serving plate. Sprinkle with peach juice from the can. Spread with raspberry jam, then add a layer of peaches and a layer of whipped cream. Put the middle cake round on top and repeat the layers of peach juice, raspberry jam, peaches and whipped cream. Finally add the bottom round of cake, upside down to give a flat top layer, and sprinkle with peach juice only.

5 Whisk the double cream and the sugar together until the cream just holds its shape. Use the cream to cover the top of the cake. Arrange the fresh fruit berries decoratively on top. Alternatively, if fresh berries are not available, decorate with more canned peaches.

This is the Norwegian celebration cake, suitable for any special occasion but especially good on the 17th May, the Norwegian national day, when the national constitution was adopted. The possibilities for the presentation of the cake are numerous and cooks pride themselves on their elaborate arrangements of fruit and whipped cream.

Serves 6–8

115g/4oz/1 cup plain (all-purpose) flour
5ml/1 tsp baking powder
4 large eggs
90g/3½oz/½ cup caster (superfine) sugar

For the filling

300ml/10fl oz/1¼ cups whipping cream
2 x 400g/14oz/2½ cups sliced peaches
raspberry jam
300ml/10fl oz/1¼ cups double (heavy) cream
5ml/1 tsp sugar
3 varieties fresh fruit berries, such as raspberries, strawberries, bilberries or blueberries, or canned peaches

Vanilla Christmas Biscuits Vaniljehjerter

Makes about 24

225g/8oz/2 cups plain (all-purpose)
   flour
5ml/1 tsp baking powder
150g/5oz/10 tbsp butter, at room
   temperature
90g/3½oz/½ cup caster (superfine)
   sugar
1 egg, lightly beaten
7.5ml/1½ tsp vanilla extract
120ml/4fl oz/½ cup milk

COOK'S TIP

A pretty finish could be provided
by brushing the hearts with lightly
beaten egg white and sprinkling
with caster sugar before baking.

*These heart-shaped treats
are a perfect choice for a
Christmas bake-in. They
are not only ideal with a
cup of tea or coffee but can
accompany a dessert such
as fruit salad. A little box of
them wrapped with a big red
bow also makes a delightful
present.*

1 Sift the flour and baking powder together. Put the butter and sugar in a large bowl and beat together until light and fluffy. Add the egg and vanilla extract, then add the milk, alternating it with the sifted flour. Mix together, then knead the dough lightly. Chill for 30 minutes.

2 Preheat the oven to 180°C/350°F/Gas 4. Butter a large baking tray. On a lightly floured surface, roll out the dough to 1cm/½in thickness. Using a heart-shaped cutter, cut out hearts and place on the prepared baking tray. Bring the pastry trimmings together, knead lightly, roll and cut out more hearts.

3 Bake the biscuits (cookies) for about 10 minutes until lightly golden brown. Leave on the tray for 2–3 minutes, then transfer to a wire rack and leave to cool.

Thin Potato Bread Lefse

Makes about 35

1kg/2¼lb potatoes
40g/1½oz/3 tbsp butter
120ml/4fl oz/½ cup single (light)
  cream
450–600g/1–1⅓lb/4–5 cups plain
  (all-purpose) flour
salt

A traditional Norwegian bread, the many types of lefse are all very thin, slightly soft breads. They can be eaten buttered and sprinkled with sugar or served with honey, lingonberry or cloudberry jam. Lefse can also be wrapped around a hotdog or filled with meat or fish and a salad.

1 Peel and cut the potatoes. Bring to the boil in a pan of salted water and simmer for about 20 minutes until tender. Drain and put through a ricer or a sieve (strainer) into a large bowl. Add the butter, cream and 5ml/1 tsp salt and beat together. Leave to cool.

2 When the potatoes are cool, add enough flour to form a firm dough. On a lightly floured surface, knead until smooth. Divide the dough into pieces about the size of a large egg, roll into balls and put on a baking tray. Chill in the refrigerator for 30 minutes.

3 On a floured surface, roll out each ball of dough very thinly. Heat a large ungreased frying pan or griddle and cook the breads over a medium heat, one at a time, until brown spots appear on the surface. Turn and cook the second side. Put the breads between two dish towels to stop them from drying out. Serve immediately.

Tosca Cake Toscakake

1 Preheat the oven to 160°C/325°F/Gas 3. Butter and line the base and sides of a 20cm/8in round cake tin (pan) with baking parchment. Melt the butter and leave to cool. Sift together the flour, baking powder and salt.

2 In a large bowl, whisk the eggs until thick and pale and then gradually whisk in the sugar until the mixture falls in a thick ribbon. Fold in the flour mixture and the cooled butter.

3 Pour the mixture into the prepared tin and tap lightly on a work surface to settle the mixture. Bake the cake in the oven for 30 minutes, or until just before the cake is cooked, when it is almost firm to the touch but needs another few minutes not to sink if removed from the heat.

4 Leave the cake in the oven and prepare the topping. Place the butter, almonds, sugar, flour and cream or milk in a pan and heat gently, stirring, until the butter has melted, then continue heating the mixture until it just reaches boiling point.

5 Preheat the grill (broiler) to medium-hot. Remove the cake carefully from the oven and spread the topping over the top, making sure that all the cake is covered. Place under the grill until the topping is golden brown, watching that the sides of the cake don't burn. Stand the tin on a rack so that air can pass underneath, and leave to cool before carefully removing the cake from the tin.

Serves 10

50g/2oz/4 tbsp unsalted butter, plus extra for greasing
115g/4oz/1 cup plain (all-purpose) flour
7.5ml/1½ tsp baking powder
pinch of salt
2 large eggs
150g/5oz/¾ cup caster (superfine) sugar

For the topping

115g/4oz/½ cup butter, softened
150g/5oz/1¼ cups blanched almonds, toasted and roughly chopped
115g/4oz/generous ½ cup caster (superfine) sugar
30ml/2 tbsp plain (all-purpose) flour
30ml/2 tbsp single (light) cream or milk

Almonds are very popular throughout Scandinavia and tosca cake uses them in a wonderful, irresistible topping. The cake is a guaranteed success on any coffee or tea table. The following recipe is my mother's, and it has more topping than the more classic version. If you prefer, use half the amount of topping for a lighter effect.

Cardamom Buns Juleboller

Makes 24

350ml/12fl oz/1½ cups milk
1 packet dried yeast
75g/3oz/6 tbsp caster (superfine)
    sugar, plus 2.5ml/½ tsp caster
    sugar
450g/1lb/4 cups strong white bread
    flour
2.5ml/½ tsp salt
10ml/2 tsp cardamom seeds, well
    crushed
115g/4oz/½ cup butter, melted
beaten egg, to glaze

COOK'S TIP

In Norway, on the first Sunday in Lent, these buns are cut in half, filled with whipped cream and the tops covered in sifted icing (confectioner's) sugar to be served as a dessert.

Norwegian children have been brought up on these buns. This is an example of Norway's fondness for the very distinctive flavour of cardamom.

1 Line a baking tray with baking parchment. Bring the milk to just below boiling point. Pour into a jug (pitcher) and leave until warm. Sprinkle in the yeast and the 2.5ml/½ tsp sugar and leave for 15 minutes until frothy.

2 Put the flour in a large bowl, add the rest of the sugar, salt and crushed cardamom seeds and mix well together. Add the milk mixture and the melted butter to the flour mixture and mix together to make a stiff dough.

3 Knead the dough on a floured surface until it feels firm and elastic. Put the dough in a bowl, cover with a damp dish towel and leave in a warm place to double in size. Turn the dough on to a lightly floured surface, knock down and knead for 2–3 minutes. Divide the dough into 24 equal pieces and shape each one into a ball. Put on the baking tray and leave to rise for about 20 minutes until nearly doubled in size.

4 Preheat the oven to 230°C/450°F/Gas 8. Brush the buns with beaten egg and bake in the oven for about 8 minutes until golden brown.

Nutritional notes

Herrings with Carrot and Leek: Energy 174kcal/731kJ; Protein 13.2g; Carbohydrate 10.9g, of which sugars 10.3g; Fat 8.5g, of which saturates 0.1g; Cholesterol 32mg; Calcium 24mg; Fibre 1.2g; Sodium 628mg.

Salted Herrings in Sherry: Energy 228kcal/960kJ; Protein 12.8g; Carbohydrate 20.7g, of which sugars 20.4g; Fat 8.4g, of which saturates 0g; Cholesterol 32mg; Calcium 21mg; Fibre 0.2g; Sodium 626mg.

Marinated Salmon: Energy 479kcal/1981kJ; Protein 26.3g; Carbohydrate 0.4g, of which sugars 0.3g; Fat 40.4g, of which saturates 6.4g; Cholesterol 113mg; Calcium 35mg; Fibre 0g; Sodium 169mg.

Liver Pâté: Energy 588kcal/2433kJ; Protein 21.4g; Carbohydrate 1.85g, of which sugars 1.6g; Fat 55.2g, of which saturates 23.9g; Cholesterol 344mg; Calcium 52mg; Fibre 0.1g; Sodium 202mg.

Wild Mushroom Soup: Energy 154kcal/638kJ; Protein 3.2g; Carbohydrate 9.3g, of which sugars 0.5g; Fat 11.8g, of which saturates 7.2g; Cholesterol 29mg; Calcium 26mg; Fibre 1.6g; Sodium 82mg.

Juniper and Apple Soup: Energy 406kcal/1677kJ; Protein 1.4g; Carbohydrate 8.5g, of which sugars 8.1g; Fat 39.2g, of which saturates 21.7g; Cholesterol 86mg; Calcium 48mg; Fibre 1.2g; Sodium 29mg.

Curry Soup: Energy 195kcal/812kJ; Protein 1.7g; Carbohydrate 14.3g, of which sugars 7.6g; Fat 15g, of which saturates 9.2g; Cholesterol 37mg; Calcium 66mg; Fibre 1.3g; Sodium 200mg.

Salmon Rolls with Asparagus and Butter Sauce: Energy 694kcal/2867kJ; Protein 25.7g; Carbohydrate 2.4g, of which sugars 2.1g; Fat 62.5g, of which saturates 33.4g; Cholesterol 187mg; Calcium 55mg; Fibre 0.6g; Sodium 362mg.

Pollock with Onions: Energy 298kcal/1247kJ; Protein 32.9g; Carbohydrate 16g, of which sugars 5g; Fat 11.8g, of which saturates 6.7g; Cholesterol 104mg; Calcium 52mg; Fibre 1.3g; Sodium 180mg.

Shellfish Salad: Energy 280kcal/1166kJ; Protein 23.2g; Carbohydrate 4.4g, of which sugars 3g; Fat 19g, of which saturates 2.9g; Cholesterol 127mg; Calcium 96mg; Fibre 1.8g; Sodium 357mg.

Crisp Fried Herrings: Energy 427kcal/1788kJ; Protein 23.9g; Carbohydrate 32.1g, of which sugars 1g; Fat 23.5g, of which saturates 8.9g; Cholesterol 119mg; Calcium 124mg; Fibre 1g; Sodium 417mg.

Salted Cod Casserole: Energy 590kcal/2484kJ; Protein 83.7g; Carbohydrate 21.9g, of which sugars 3.1g; Fat 19.2g, of which saturates 3g; Cholesterol 148mg; Calcium 68mg; Fibre 1.7g; Sodium 1016mg.

Beef Meatballs in Gravy: Energy 454kcal/1882kJ; Protein 26.9g; Carbohydrate 5g, of which sugars 0.3g; Fat 36.4g, of which saturates 15.5g; Cholesterol 146mg; Calcium 32mg; Fibre 0.2g; Sodium 157mg.

Lamb and Cabbage: Energy 390kcal/1630kJ; Protein 37.6g; Carbohydrate 16.3g, of which sugars 15.9g; Fat 19.6g, of which saturates 8.8g; Cholesterol 128mg; Calcium 173mg; Fibre 6.8g; Sodium 168mg.

Fried Pork and Apples: Energy 645kcal/2676kJ; Protein 23.4g; Carbohydrate 19g, of which sugars 19g; Fat 53.4g, of which saturates 19.7g; Cholesterol 108mg; Calcium 21mg; Fibre 2g; Sodium 113mg.

Roast Pork Loin with Red Cabbage: Energy 416kcal/1749kJ; Protein 55.8g; Carbohydrate 20g, of which sugars 19.8g; Fat 12.9g, of which saturates 5.1g; Cholesterol 164mg; Calcium 96mg; Fibre 3.8g; Sodium 209mg.

Braised Chicken with Mashed Swede: Energy 821kcal/3410kJ; Protein 43.5g; Carbohydrate 33g, of which sugars 7.9g; Fat 58g, of which saturates 24.9g; Cholesterol 269mg; Calcium 91mg; Fibre 3.8g; Sodium 372mg.

Reindeer Terrine: Energy 492kcal/2039kJ; Protein 26.8g; Carbohydrate 0.4g, of which sugars 0.4g; Fat 41.4g, of which saturates 18.6g; Cholesterol 123mg; Calcium 22mg; Fibre 0g; Sodium 322mg.

Roe Deer Medallions with Redcurrants: Energy 337kcal/1407kJ; Protein 30.1g; Carbohydrate 3.8g, of which sugars 3.8g; Fat 20.3g, of which saturates 10.9g; Cholesterol 106mg; Calcium 23mg; Fibre 0.2g; Sodium 95mg.

Pheasant Stuffed with Mountain Fruits: Energy 213kcal/893kJ; Protein 21.3g; Carbohydrate 8.6g, of which sugars 8.6g; Fat 10g, of which saturates 4.5g; Cholesterol 12mg; Calcium 58mg; Fibre 1.7g; Sodium 85mg.

Norwegian Pancakes: Energy 105kcal/438kJ; Protein 3.5g; Carbohydrate 8.8g, of which sugars 1.5g; Fat 6.5g, of which saturates 2.1g; Cholesterol 54mg; Calcium 56mg; Fibre 0.3g; Sodium 43mg.

Rhubarb Soup: Energy 179kcal/765kJ; Protein 1.4g; Carbohydrate 46g, of which sugars 40.2g; Fat 0.2g, of which saturates 0g; Cholesterol 0mg; Calcium 137mg; Fibre 1.8g; Sodium 9mg.

Peasant Girls in a Veil: Energy 813kcal/3380kJ; Protein 7.3g; Carbohydrate 50g, of which sugars 37.5g; Fat 66.4g, of which saturates 37.6g; Cholesterol 153mg; Calcium 123mg; Fibre 5.3g; Sodium 327mg.

Caramel Pudding: Energy 296kcal/1248kJ; Protein 13.1g; Carbohydrate 37.1g, of which sugars 37.1g; Fat 11.8g, of which saturates 4.2g; Cholesterol 337mg; Calcium 239mg; Fibre 0g; Sodium 136mg.

Cream Layer Cake: Energy 363kcal/1513kJ; Protein 5.7g; Carbohydrate 35.2g, of which sugars 24.3g; Fat 23.1g, of which saturates 13.3g; Cholesterol 147mg; Calcium 64mg; Fibre 1.3g; Sodium 57mg.

Vanilla Christmas Biscuits: Energy 100kcal/420kJ; Protein 1.4g; Carbohydrate 11.9g, of which sugars 4.8g; Fat 5.6g, of which saturates 3.4g; Cholesterol 22mg; Calcium 24mg; Fibre 0.3g; Sodium 43mg.

Thin Potato Bread: Energy 71kcal/301kJ; Protein 1.8g; Carbohydrate 14.7g, of which sugars 0.6g; Fat 1g, of which saturates 0.5g; Cholesterol 2mg; Calcium 23mg; Fibre 0.7g; Sodium 5mg.

Tosca Cake: Energy 389kcal/1626kJ; Protein 6.1g; Carbohydrate 40.2g, of which sugars 28.7g; Fat 23g, of which saturates 10g; Cholesterol 75mg; Calcium 82mg; Fibre 1.5g; Sodium 119mg.

Cardamom Buns: Energy 119kcal/499kJ; Protein 2.3g; Carbohydrate 18.6g, of which sugars 4.3g; Fat 4.4g, of which saturates 2.7g; Cholesterol 11mg; Calcium 46mg; Fibre 0.6g; Sodium 36mg.

Index